I0412174

United States
Department of
Agriculture

Forest Service

**Northern
Research Station**

General Technical
Report NRS-30

A Simplified Forest Inventory and Analysis Database: FIADB-Lite

Patrick D. Miles

Abstract

U.S. Forest Service Forest Inventory and Analysis (FIA) data are stored in the Forest Inventory and Analysis Database (FIADB). FIADB-Lite was developed to simplify the generation of forest statistics. An FIADB-Lite database can be used to generate estimates of forest land area and tree biomass, volume, growth, removals, and mortality. FIADB-Lite consists of five database tables: four tables currently in the FIADB (POP_EVAL_GRP, COND, TREE, and SEEDLING) that are described in the FIADB Users Guide Version 3.0 (Conkling, editor, draft), and one new table, PLOTSNAP.

The PLOTSNAP table combines information from three FIADB tables (PLOT, POP_ EVAL_GRP, and POP_STRATUM) to provide a "snapshot" of the PLOT records and their associated expansion and adjustment factors that were used to produce a state inventory report. Combining information from these three tables greatly simplifies the procedures for generating forest statistics. Users needing associated sampling errors should use the entire FIADB rather than FIADB-Lite because calculation of variances requires information from additional tables.

FIADB-Lite download files and an MS-Access database with stored Data Import Specifications and stored Queries for generating population estimates are available from the FIA national web site (www.fia.fs.fed.us) on the data download page.

The Authors

PATRICK D. MILES is a Research Forester with the Northern Research Station, U.S. Forest Service, 1992 Folwell Avenue, St. Paul, MN 55108.

A Simplified Forest Inventory and Analysis Database: FIADB-Lite

Patrick D. Miles
U.S. Forest Service
Northern Research Station

Contents

INTRODUCTION

This publication is a companion to the FIADB Users Guide Version 3.0 (Conkling, editor, draft). The FIADB (Forest Inventory and Analysis Data Base) format contains all the information needed to produce population estimates and their associated sampling errors. Some FIA data users, however, may not be interested in sampling errors or, for that matter, population estimates. These users will find the FIADB unnecessarily complex.

GIS specialists, for example, may be interested only in identifying and retrieving geographic information and per acre values for the set of plots used in producing forest statistics for a state report. To identify this set of plots using the FIADB, users must join records from six tables (POP_EVAL_GRP, POP_EVAL, POP_ESTN_UNIT, POP_STRATUM, POP_PLOT_STRATUM_ASSGN, and PLOT).

Application developers and modelers may also find the FIADB to be overly complex. While this level of complexity is required for computing sampling errors, it is not necessary for computing population estimates. Much of the complexity can be stripped away if sampling errors are not needed.

FIADB-Lite was designed for these users. The set of plots used in producing forest statistics for a state report can be identified via a single variable (EVAL_GRP) found on the PLOTSNAP table. Data processing has also been simplified by combining information found in three tables into a single table (PLOTSNAP).

Examples for generating population estimates from the FIADB-Lite format are written in the Structured Query Language (SQL) for Microsoft Access and Oracle.

FIADB-LITE DATABASE STRUCTURE

The FIADB-Lite database consists of five tables briefly described in Table 1. Four of these tables (POP_EVAL_GRP, COND, TREE, and SEEDLING) replicate tables from the FIADB and are fully documented elsewhere (Conkling, editor, draft). The fifth table (PLOTSNAP), described fully in Appendix A, combines data found in FIADB tables PLOT, POP_EVAL_GRP, and POP_STRATUM.

Table 1.—FIADB-Lite table descriptions

Table Name	Description
POP_EVAL_GRP	Each record in the POP_EVAL_GRP table corresponds to a state inventory report. For example, there are currently six POP_EVAL_GRP records for the State of Michigan: 1) the 1980 periodic inventory 2) the 1993 periodic inventory 3) the 2000-2003 rolling average annual inventory 4) the 2000-2004 rolling average annual inventory 5) the 2001-2005 rolling average annual inventory 6) the 2002-2006 rolling average annual inventory Each of these inventories can be uniquely identified in the POP_EVAL_GRP table by two variables (STATECD and EVAL_GRP).
PLOTSNAP	Provides information relevant to the entire 1-acre field plot. Similar to the PLOT table in the FIADB except that it includes an EVAL_GRP variable allowing the PLOTSNAP record to be directly linked to the corresponding record in the POP_EVAL_GRP table. The PLOTSNAP table also contains expansion and adjustment factors to identify the number of acres the sample plot represented in the state inventory for area, volume, growth, removals, and mortality. There will be one or more COND records for each PLOTSNAP record.
COND	Provides information on the discrete combination of landscape attributes that define the condition (a condition will have the same land class, reserved status, owner group, forest type, stand-size class, regeneration status, and stand density). Can be linked to plot record where cond.plt_cn=plot.cn.
TREE	Describes each tree 1 inch in diameter and larger found on a microplot or subplot. Can be linked to plot record where tree.plt_cn=plot.cn.
SEEDLING	Provides a count of the number of live trees of a species found on a microplot that are less than 1 inch in diameter but at least 6 inches in length for conifer species or at least 12 inches in length for hardwood species. Can be linked to plot record where seedling.plt_cn=plot.cn.

DOWNLOADING FIADB COMMA-DELIMITED DATA

FIADB download files can now be found at: http://fiatools.fs.fed.us/fiadb-downloads/fiadb3.html. Currently 58 tables are available for downloading on this web page. Seventeen of these tables are reference or lookup tables containing information about the meaning of various numeric codes in the database. The other 41 tables, which are bundled by state into a ZIP file, contain FIA data (field data, summarized remote sensing data, and computed data). The five FIADB-Lite tables (POP_EVAL_ GRP, PLOTSNAP, COND, TREE, and SEEDLING) are included in each state bundle. It is easier to retrieve a state ZIP file containing all 41 tables than to retrieve the 5 tables individually.

Six steps are involved in downloading comma-delimited data. In this example the state ZIP file for Rhode Island will be downloaded.

Step 1. Go to the FIADB download web page at http://fiatools.fs.fed.us/fiadb-downloads/fiadb3.html and click on the state abbreviation "RI" on the map on the left side of the page (Fig. 1).

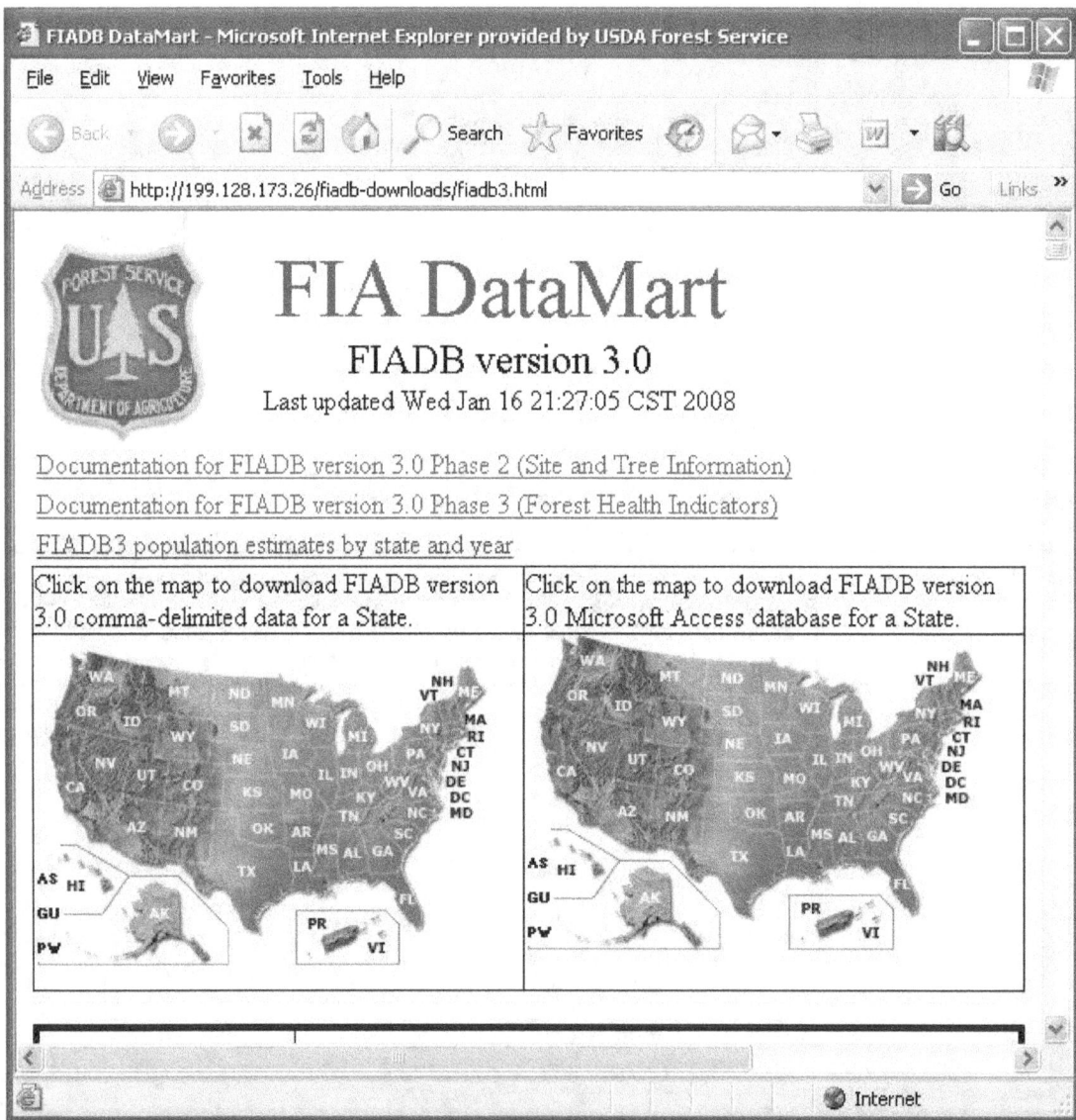

Figure 1.—Clickable map for downloading FIA data by state.

Step 2. A File Download window (Fig. 2) will appear on your screen. Click on the "Save" button.

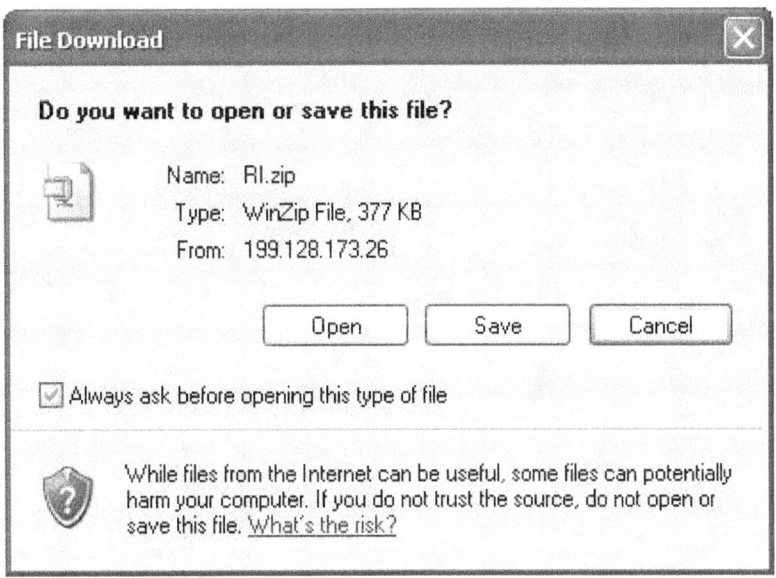

Figure 2.—File Download window.

Step 3. Save the file "RI.zip" in a folder called RI on your computer (Fig. 3). In this example the folder was saved at the root directory (C:\).

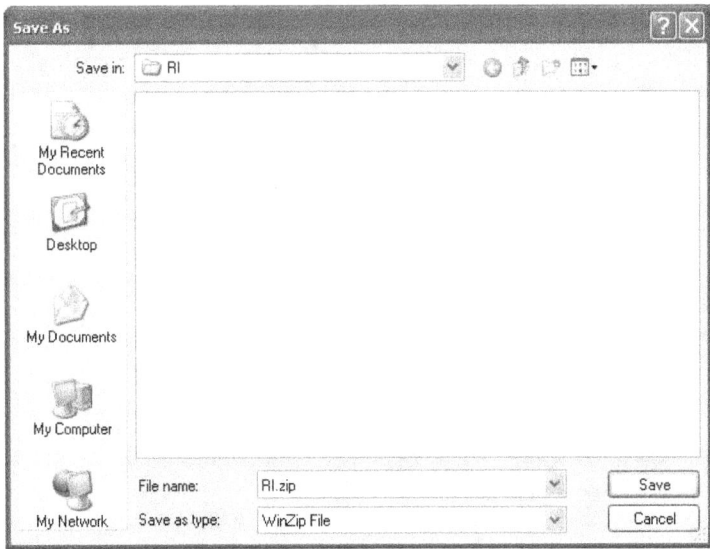

Figure 3.—Save the RI.zip file.

Step 4. Double-click on the RI.zip file (Fig. 4) to begin extracting the data files within.

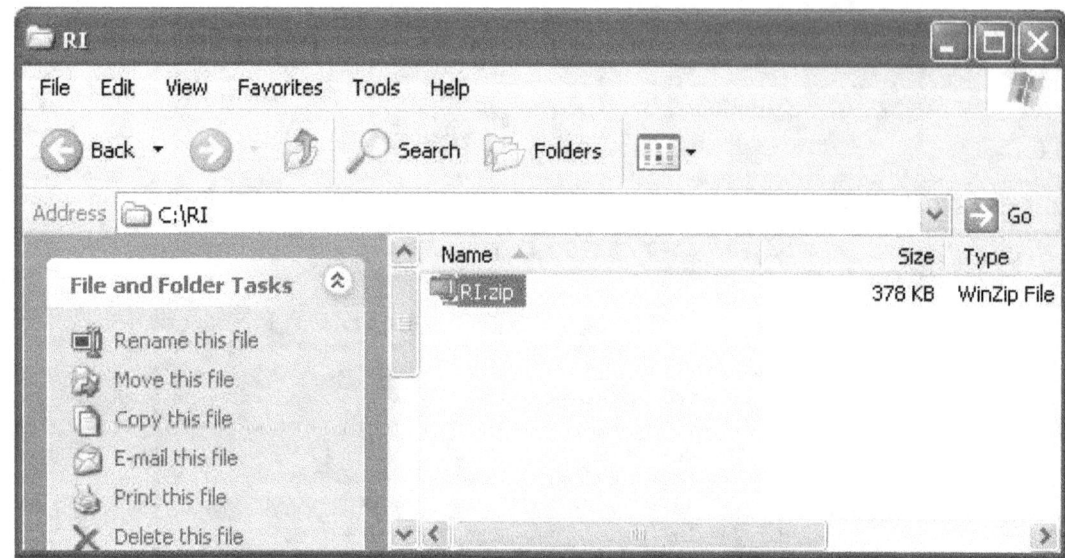

Figure 4.—Double-click on the RI.zip icon to begin extracting data from the ZIP file.

Step 5. Click on the Extract button (Fig. 5) to begin extracting all the files in the zip.

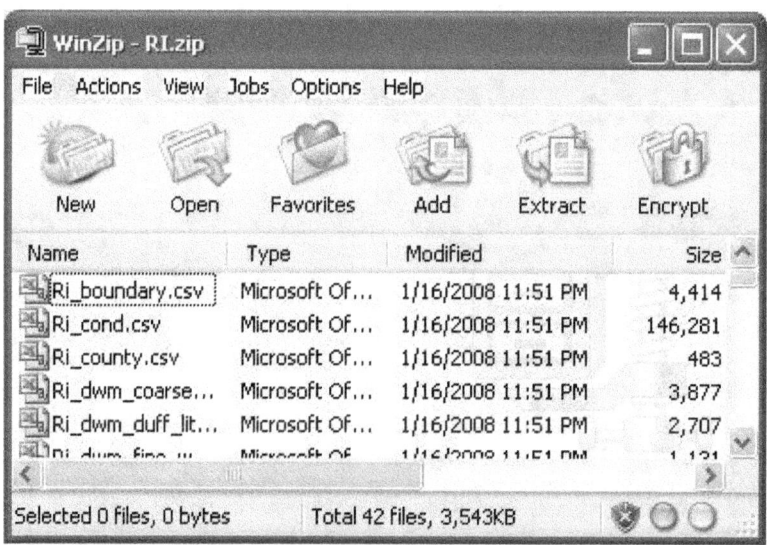

Figure 5.—Click on "Extract" button.

Step 6. The Extract window (Fig. 6) will open. Specify the folder where you want the data files to go and click on the "Extract" button. In this case we want to save the files in C:\RI.

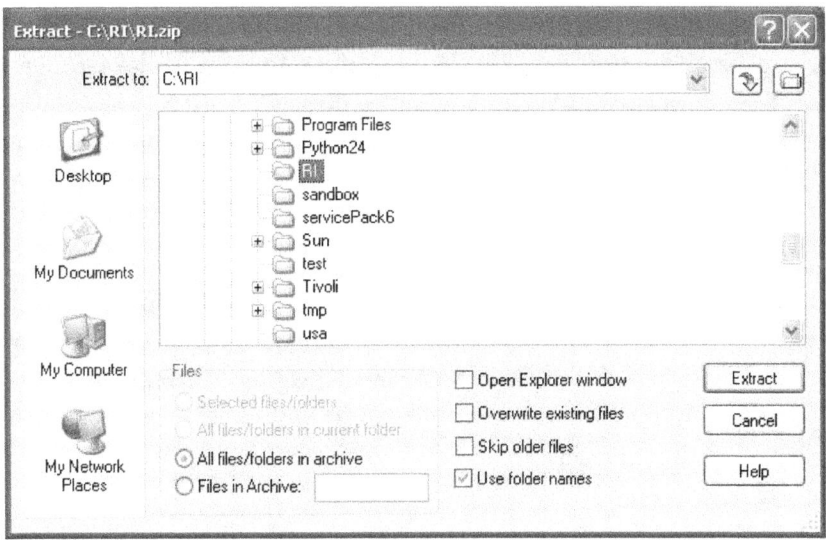

Figure 6.—Extract window.

The files should now be in the folder C:\RI.

IMPORTING FIADB DATA INTO A MICROSOFT ACCESS DATABASE

The following steps require users to have Microsoft Access software on their computers.

An MS-Access database file named Shell_FIADB_Lite.mdb is available for downloading at http://fiatools.fs.fed.us/fiadb-downloads/fiadb3.html. Click on the link labeled Microsoft Access Database file ready for loading FIADB-Lite data (empty, pre-defined tables, ready to import data) to download this file to your computer. Save this file in folder C:\RI.

The Shell_FIADB_Lite.mdb database contains 5 empty Tables, 5 Data Import Specifications, and over 40 Queries for generating population estimates and per acre values. The five tables in the database are initially empty. Data from one or more states can be imported into the database to populate these tables. Microsoft Access files cannot exceed 2 gigabytes so only a few states can be loaded into the Shell_FIADB_Lite database at one time. The following example illustrates how to populate the Shell_FIADB_Lite database.

Open the Shell_FIADB_LITE database by double-clicking on the filename "Shell_FIADB_LITE.mdb" in the C:\RI directory. The Microsoft Access database will open. There will be five empty tables in this database (Fig. 7): COND, PLOTSNAP, POP_EVAL_GRP, SEEDLING, and TREE.

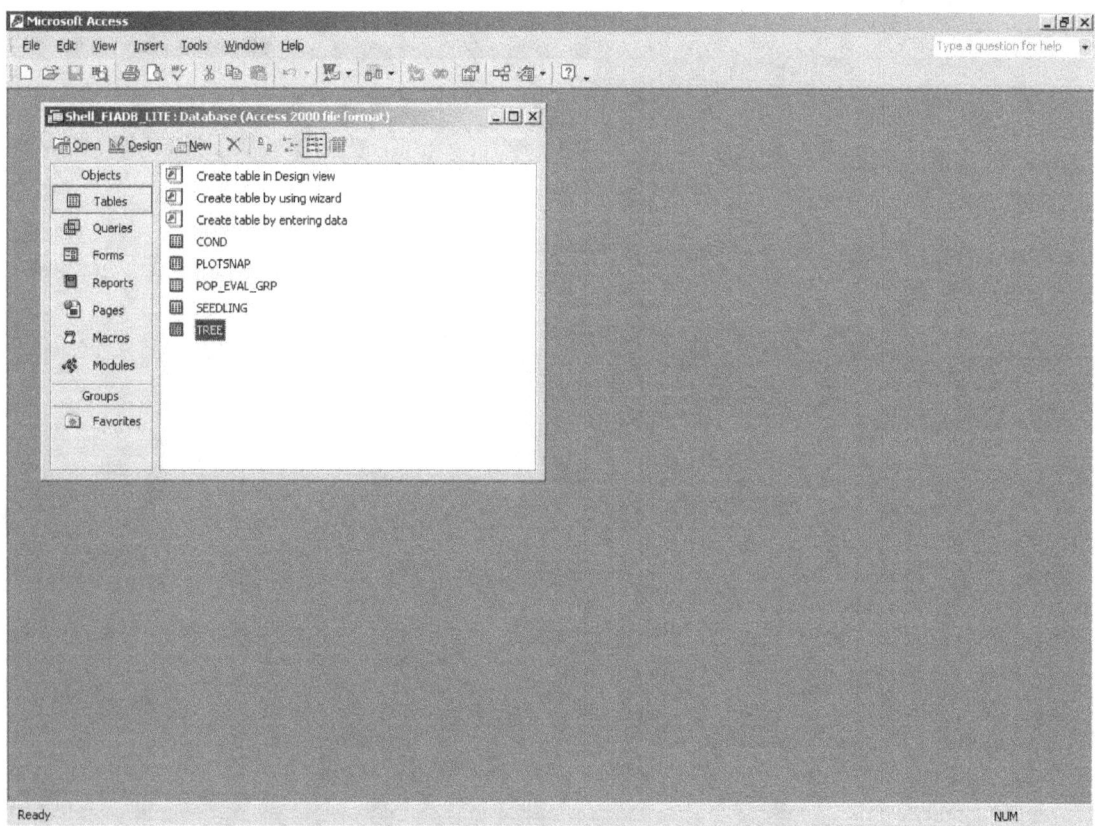

Figure 7.—Five empty tables in the Shell_FIADB_LITE database.

8

The database also has over 40 Queries (Fig. 8) that can be used to generate population estimates and per acre values.

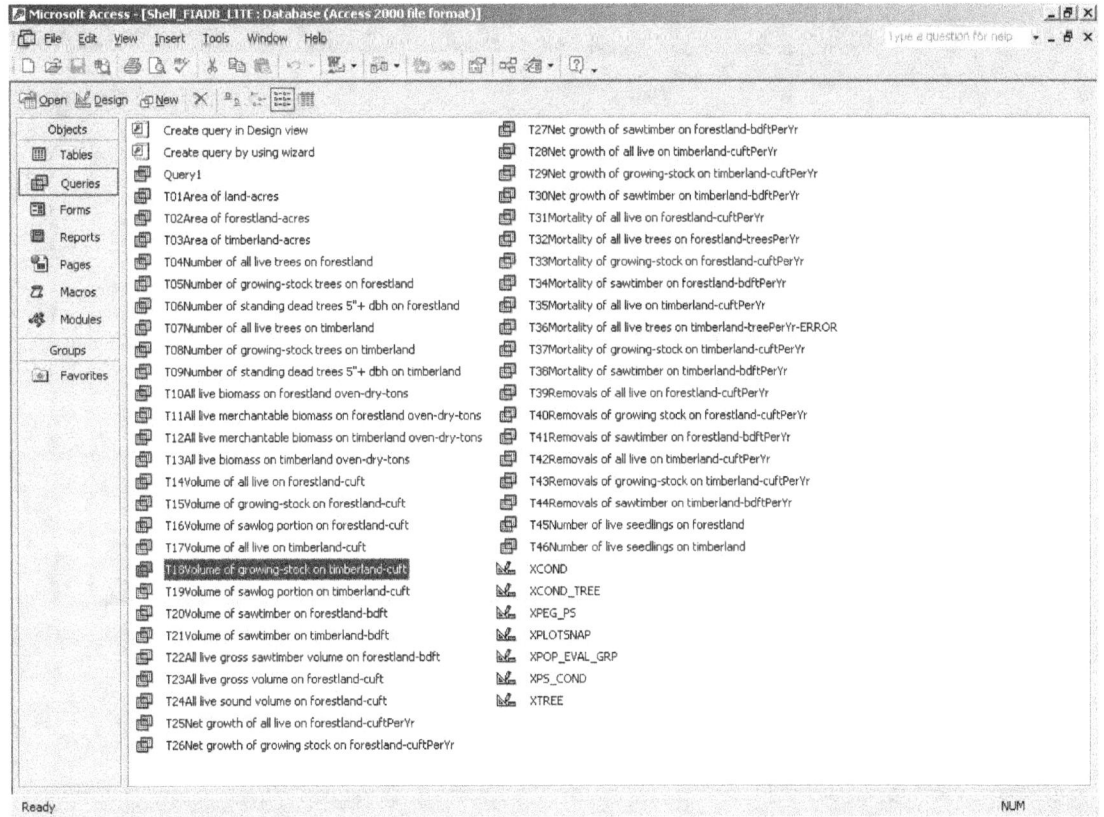

Figure 8.—Queries available in Shell_FIADB_LITE database.

Import specification files have also been created to facilitate the loading of the CSV (comma-separated values) files you have extracted. There are seven steps to importing the comma-delimited data into the Shell_FIADB_LITE database.

Step 1. Open the Shell_FIADB_LITE database and click on "Forms" (Fig. 9). Then double-click on "Import FIADB-Lite Data for a State".

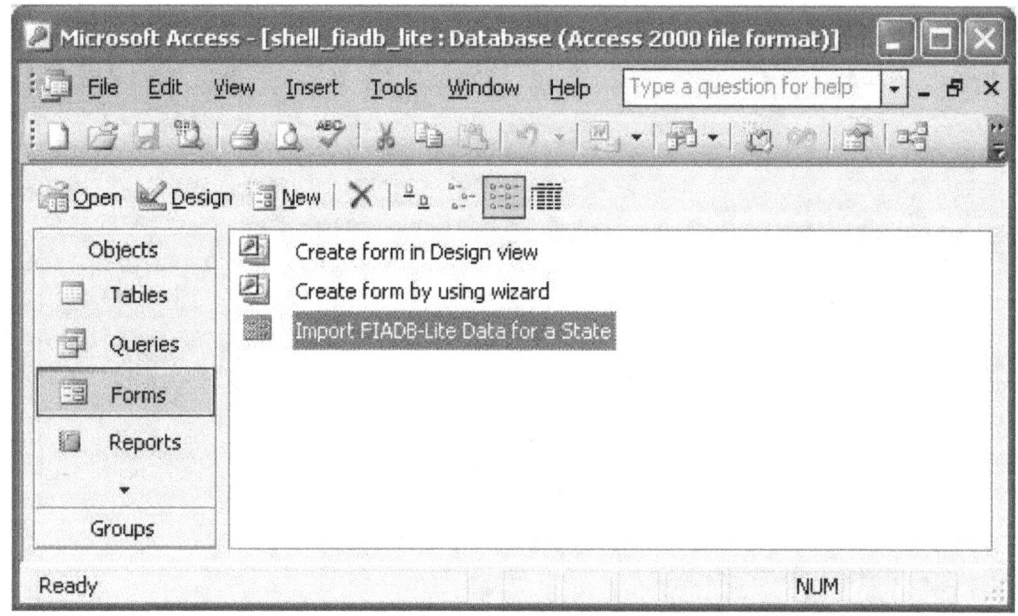

Figure 9.—Access form to load FIADB-Lite data into Access tables.

Step 2. A form will appear with one command button: "Click me to find extracted PLOTSNAP FILE and import all FIADB-Lite data" (Fig. 10). Click on this command button.

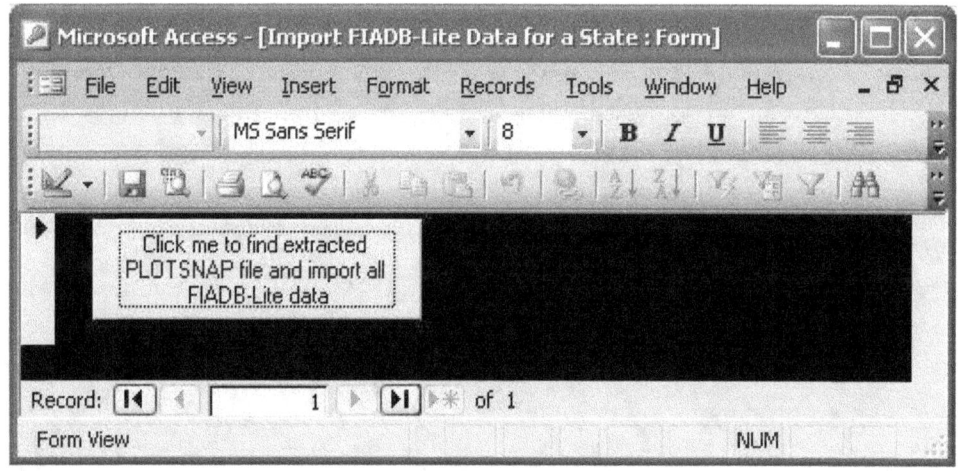

Figure 10.—Command button to begin importing data from CSV files.

Step 3. A common dialog window will appear (Fig. 11). Locate the RI_PLOTSNAP.CSV file and double-click on the filename. If the import is successful, a message box should appear. Click on the "OK" button (Fig. 12) and close the form.

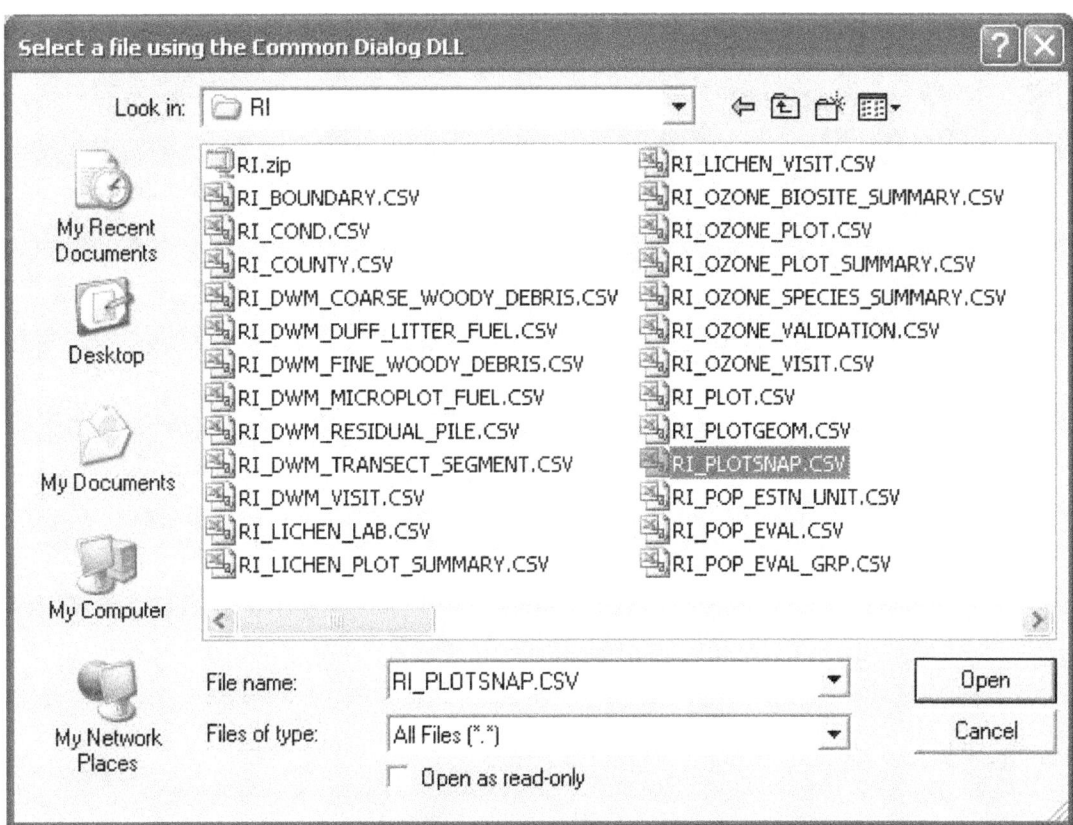

Figure 11.—Use this common dialog window to navigate to C:\RI\RI_PLOTSNAP.CSV

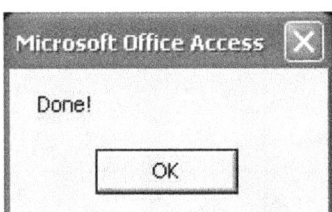

Figure 12.—Message box indicating that the import was successful.

Step 4. Then go to "Tables" and double-click on "COND" (Fig. 13).

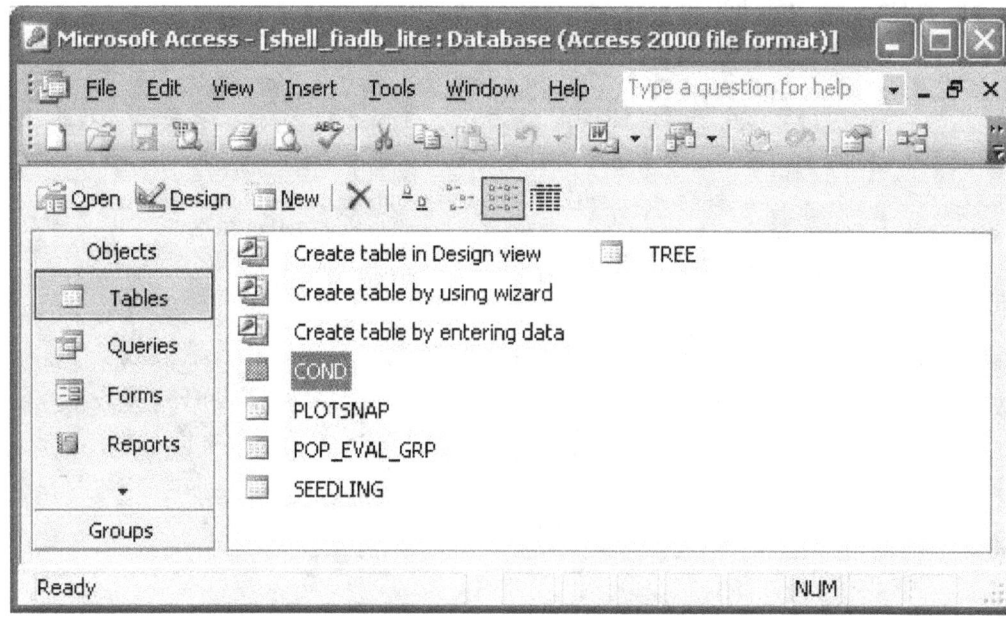

Figure 13.—Table viewing pane.

There should now be records in the COND table (Fig. 14)

CN	PLT_CN	INVYR	STATECD	UNITCD
1017889701066	1017889601066	1985	44	1
1017891701066	1017891601066	1985	44	1
1017894301066	1017894201066	1985	44	1
1017894501066	1017894401066	1985	44	1
1017898701066	1017898601066	1985	44	1
1017898901066	1017898801066	1985	44	1
1017899101066	1017899001066	1985	44	1
1017899301066	1017899201066	1985	44	1
1017902101066	1017902001066	1985	44	1

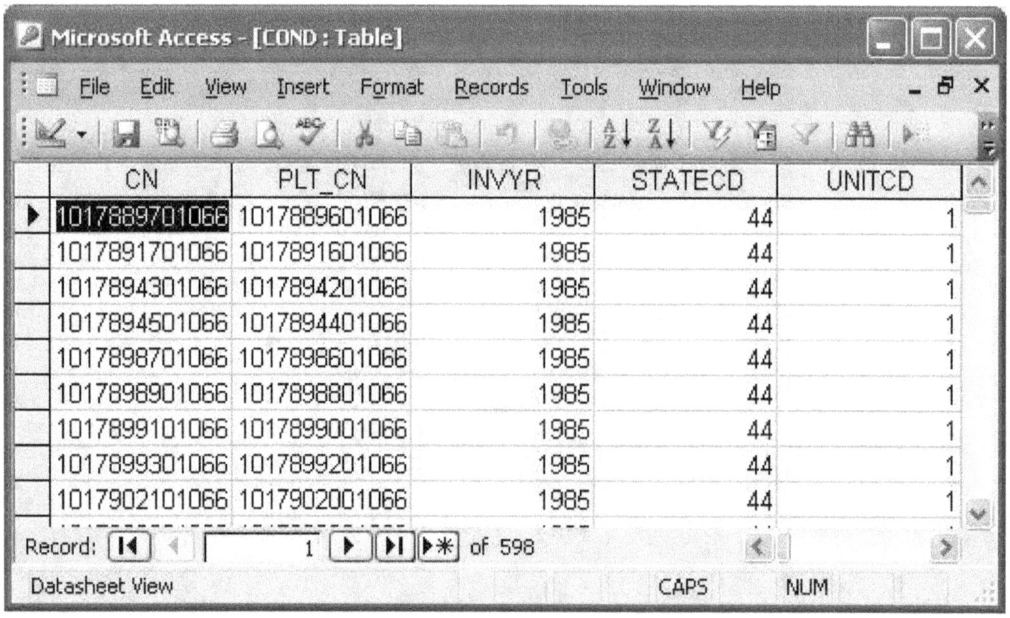

Figure 14.—COND table records.

USING THE FIADB-LITE DATABASE

Appendix B contains a listing of the population estimates, and associated Oracle SQL scripts, that can be computed using FIADB-Lite. Several examples of both Oracle and MS-Access SQL scripts are provided here.

Not all estimates can be produced for every state/inventory. Estimates of biomass, numbers of trees, volume, growth, removals, and mortality on forest land will usually be unavailable for inventories conducted before 1999 when the annual inventory sample design was implemented. For these earlier inventories, tree measurements were taken on timberland plots but not always on unproductive and reserved forest land plots. A spreadsheet providing "FIADB3 population estimates by state and year" is available at http://fiatools.fs.fed.us/fiadb-downloads/FIADB3_pop_estimates.html. This spreadsheet provides 46 population estimates for each state/inventory. A value of zero for any estimate indicates that the inventory should not be used to calculate this estimate for the indicated state/inventory.

Per Acre Estimate Examples

Proportion of plot that is forest land, Alabama 2006	

Oracle SQL	select p.cn, p.lat, p.lon, sum(c.condprop_unadj) prop_forestland
	  from pop_eval_grp peg, plotsnap p, cond c
	where c.cond_status_cd = 1
	  and p.cn = c.plt_cn
	  and peg.eval_grp = p.eval_grp
	  and peg.statecd = p.statecd
	  and peg.statecd = 1
	  and peg.eval_grp = 12006
	group by p.cn, p.lat, p.lon;

MS-Access SQL	SELECT PLOTSNAP.CN, First(PLOTSNAP.LAT) AS LAT, First(PLOTSNAP.LON) AS LON, Sum(COND.CONDPROP_UNADJ) AS [Proportion forestland] FROM POP_EVAL_GRP INNER JOIN (PLOTSNAP INNER JOIN COND ON PLOTSNAP.CN=COND.PLT_CN) ON POP_EVAL_GRP.CN=PLOTSNAP.EVAL_GRP_CN WHERE COND.COND_STATUS_CD=1 AND POP_EVAL_GRP.EVAL_GRP=12006 AND POP_EVAL_GRP.STATECD=1 GROUP BY PLOTSNAP.CN;
Output	<table><tr><td>CN</td><td>LAT</td><td>LON</td><td>PROP_FORESTLAND</td></tr><tr><td>22346696010478</td><td>34.033407</td><td>-87.822223</td><td>1</td></tr><tr><td>22346469010478</td><td>34.930357</td><td>-86.593645</td><td>0.4917</td></tr><tr><td>81668124010478</td><td>34.341840</td><td>-88.080651</td><td>1</td></tr><tr><td>81668064010478</td><td>34.561975</td><td>-88.023739</td><td>1</td></tr><tr><td>…</td><td>…</td><td>…</td><td>…</td></tr></table>

Live tree biomass per acre by forest land plot, Alabama 2006 (dry tons)	
Oracle SQL	select p.cn,p.lat,p.lon, sum(t.tpa_unadj * t.drybiot / 2000) dryTonsPerAcre from pop_eval_grp peg, plotsnap p, cond c, tree t where t.plt_cn = c.plt_cn and t.condid = c.condid and c.cond_status_cd = 1 and t.statuscd = 1 and p.cn = c.plt_cn and peg.eval_grp = p.eval_grp and peg.statecd = p.statecd and peg.statecd = 1 and peg.eval_grp = 12006 group by p.cn,p.lat,p.lon;
MS-Access SQL	SELECT PLOTSNAP.CN, First(PLOTSNAP.LAT) AS LAT, First(PLOTSNAP.LON) AS LON, Sum([DRYBIOT]/2000*[TPA_UNADJ]) AS DryTonsPerAcre FROM POP_EVAL_GRP INNER JOIN ((PLOTSNAP INNER JOIN COND ON PLOTSNAP.CN = COND.PLT_CN) INNER JOIN TREE ON (COND.CONDID = TREE.CONDID) AND (COND.PLT_CN = TREE.PLT_CN)) ON POP_EVAL_GRP.CN = PLOTSNAP.EVAL_GRP_CN WHERE POP_EVAL_GRP.STATECD=1 AND POP_EVAL_GRP.EVAL_GRP=12006 AND COND.COND_STATUS_CD=1 AND TREE.STATUSCD=1 GROUP BY PLOTSNAP.CN;
Output	

CN	LAT	LON	DRYTONSPERACRE
22346696010478	34.033407	-87.822223	35.6578567
22346469010478	34.930357	-86.593645	72.87423088
81668124010478	34.341840	-88.080651	46.33913154
81668064010478	34.561975	-88.023739	2.568083244
…	…	…	…

Population Estimate Examples

Forest land area 2006 inventory of Alabama	
Oracle SQL	select g.eval_grp_descr, sum(expcurr * condprop_unadj * adj_expcurr) acres from plotsnap p, cond c, pop_eval_grp g where c.cond_status_cd = 1 and c.plt_cn = p.cn and p.eval_grp = g.eval_grp and p.statecd = g.statecd and p.eval_grp = 12006 and p.statecd = 1 group by g.eval_grp_descr
MS-Access SQL	SELECT POP_EVAL_GRP.EVAL_GRP_DESCR, Sum([EXPCURR]*[CONDPROP_UNADJ]*[ADJ_EXPCURR]) AS [Area of forestland-acres] FROM POP_EVAL_GRP INNER JOIN (PLOTSNAP INNER JOIN COND ON PLOTSNAP.CN = COND.PLT_CN) ON POP_EVAL_GRP.CN = PLOTSNAP.EVAL_GRP_CN WHERE PLOTSNAP.STATECD=1 AND PLOTSNAP.EVAL_GRP=12006 AND COND.COND_STATUS_CD=1 GROUP BY POP_EVAL_GRP.EVAL_GRP_DESCR;
Output	

EVAL_GRP_DESCR	ACRES
Alabama: 2001-2006: Annual - Moving Avg - 9th Survey 1 panel (4) + 8th Survey	22566073.34

Volume of growing stock on timberland 2006 inventory of Alabama	

Oracle SQL	select peg.eval_grp_descr,
	    sum(t.tpa_unadj * t.volcfnet * expvol *
	    decode(dia,null,adj_expvol_subp,
	  decode(least(dia,5-0.001),dia,adj_cxpvol_micr,
	  decode(least(dia,
	    nvl(MACRO_BREAKPOINT_DIA,9999)-0.001),
	    dia,adj_expvol_subp,
	    adj_expvol_macr)))) CUFT
	 from pop_eval_grp peg, plotsnap p, cond c, tree t
	 where t.plt_cn = c.plt_cn
	  and t.condid = c.condid
	  and c.cond_status_cd = 1
	  and c.reservcd = 0
	  and c.siteclcd in (1, 2, 3, 4, 5, 6)
	  and t.statuscd = 1
	  and t.treeclcd = 2
	  and p.cn = c.plt_cn
	  and peg.eval_grp = p.eval_grp
	  and peg.statecd = p.statecd
	  and peg.statecd = 1 and peg.eval_grp = 12006
	 group by peg.eval_grp_descr;

MS-Access SQL	SELECT POP_EVAL_GRP.EVAL_GRP_DESCR, Sum([EXPVOL]*[VOLCFNET]*[TPA_UNADJ]* IIf(IsNull([dia]),[adj_expvol_subp], IIf([dia]<5,[adj_expvol_micr], IIf(IsNull([MACRO_BREAKPOINT_DIA]),[adj_expvol_subp], IIf([dia]<[MACRO_BREAKPOINT_DIA],[adj_expvol_subp],[adj_expvol_macr]))))) AS [Volume of growing stock on timberland-cuft] FROM POP_EVAL_GRP INNER JOIN ((PLOTSNAP INNER JOIN COND ON PLOTSNAP.CN = COND.PLT_CN) INNER JOIN TREE ON (COND.PLT_CN = TREE.PLT_CN) AND (COND.CONDID = TREE.CONDID)) ON POP_EVAL_GRP.CN = PLOTSNAP.EVAL_GRP_CN WHERE (((TREE.TREECLCD)=2) AND ((COND.COND_STATUS_CD)=1) AND ((TREE.STATUSCD)=1) AND ((COND.RESERVCD)=0) AND ((COND.SITECLCD)=1 Or (COND.SITECLCD)=2 Or (COND.SITECLCD)=3 Or (COND.SITECLCD)=4 Or (COND.SITECLCD)=5 Or (COND.SITECLCD)=6)) GROUP BY POP_EVAL_GRP.EVAL_GRP_DESCR;
Output	EVAL_GRP_DESCR CUFT Alabama: 2001-2006: Annual - Moving Avg - 9th Survey 1 panel (4) + 8th Survey 28450849601

APPENDIX A—PLOTSNAP TABLE DESCRIPTION

The PLOTSNAP table was created to simplify the FIADB for users who want an easier way to generate population estimates and are not concerned with determining associated sampling errors. The PLOTSNAP table combines all the information in the PLOT table with information in the POP_EVAL_GRP table and the POP_STRATUM table to provide a snapshot of the plot records with their associated expansion and adjustment factors used for each state inventory report. The PLOTSNAP table has 74 variables: the first 52 variables came from the FIADB PLOT table and the last 22 came from the FIADB POP_EVAL_GRP and POP_STRATUM tables.

	Column name	Oracle Data Type	FIADB table.variable where data were obtained
1	CN	VARCHAR2(34)	PLOT.CN
2	SRV_CN	VARCHAR2(34)	PLOT.SRV_CN
3	CTY_CN	VARCHAR2(34)	PLOT.CTY_CN
4	PREV_PLT_CN	VARCHAR2(34)	PLOT.PREV_PLT_CN
5	INVYR	NUMBER(4)	PLOT.INVYR
6	STATECD	NUMBER(4)	PLOT.STATECD
7	UNITCD	NUMBER(2)	PLOT.UNITCD
8	COUNTYCD	NUMBER(3)	PLOT.COUNTYCD
9	PLOT	NUMBER(5)	PLOT.PLOT
10	PLOT_STATUS_CD	NUMBER(1)	PLOT.PLOT_STATUS_CD
11	PLOT_NONSAMPLE_REASN_CD	NUMBER(2)	PLOT.PLOT_NONSAMPLE_REASN_CD
12	MEASYEAR	NUMBER(4)	PLOT.MEASYEAR
13	MEASMON	NUMBER(2)	PLOT.MEASMON
14	MEASDAY	NUMBER(2)	PLOT.MEASDAY
15	REMPER	NUMBER(3,1)	PLOT.REMPER
16	KINDCD	NUMBER(2)	PLOT.KINDCD
17	DESIGNCD	NUMBER(4)	PLOT.DESIGNCD
18	RDDISTCD	NUMBER(2)	PLOT.RDDISTCD
19	WATERCD	NUMBER(2)	PLOT.WATERCD
20	LAT	NUMBER(8,6)	PLOT.LAT
21	LON	NUMBER(9,6)	PLOT.LON
22	ELEV	NUMBER(5)	PLOT.ELEV
23	GROWCD	NUMBER(2)	PLOT.GROWCD
24	MORTCD	NUMBER(2)	PLOT.MORTCD
25	P2PANEL	NUMBER(2)	PLOT.P2PANEL
26	P3PANEL	NUMBER(2)	PLOT.P3PANEL
27	ECOSUBCD	VARCHAR2(7)	PLOT.ECOSUBCD
28	CONGCD	NUMBER(4)	PLOT.CONGCD
29	MANUAL	NUMBER(31)	PLOT.MANUAL
30	SUBPANEL	NUMBER(2)	PLOT.SUBPANEL
31	KINDCD_NC	NUMBER(2)	PLOT.KINDCD_NC
32	QA_STATUS	NUMBER(1)	PLOT.QA_STATUS
33	CREW_TYPE	NUMBER(1)	PLOT.CREW_TYPE
34	MANUAL_DB	NUMBER(31)	PLOT.MANUAL_DB
35	CREATED_BY	VARCHAR2(30)	PLOT.CREATED_BY

36	CREATED_DATE	DATE	PLOT.CREATED_DATE
37	CREATED_IN_INSTANCE	NUMBER(6)	PLOT.CREATED_IN_INSTANCE
38	MODIFIED_BY	VARCHAR2(30)	PLOT.MODIFIED_BY
39	MODIFIED_DATE	DATF	PLOT.MODIFIED_DATE
40	MODIFIED_IN_INSTANCE	NUMBER(6)	PLOT.MODIFIED_IN_INSTANCE
41	MICROPLOT_LOC	VARCHAR2(12)	PLOT.MICROPLOT_LOC
42	DECLINATION	NUMBER(41)	PLOT.DECLINATION
43	EMAP_HEX	NUMBER(7)	PLOT.EMAP_HEX
44	REPLACED_PLOT_NBR	NUMBER(5)	PLOT.REPLACED_PLOT_NBR
45	SAMP_METHOD_CD	NUMBER(1)	PLOT.SAMP_METHOD_CD
46	SUBP_EXAMINE_CD	NUMBER(1)	PLOT.SUBP_EXAMINE_CD
47	MACRO_BREAKPOINT_DIA	NUMBER(2)	PLOT.MACRO_BREAKPOINT_DIA
48	LAST_INVYR_MEASURED	NUMBER(4)	PLOT.LAST_INVYR_MEASURED
49	CYCLE	NUMBER(2)	PLOT.CYCLE
50	SUBCYCLE	NUMBER(2)	PLOT.SUBCYCLE
51	ECO_UNIT_PNW	VARCHAR2(10)	PLOT.ECO_UNIT_PNW
52	TOPO_POSITION_PNW	VARCHAR2(2)	PLOT.TOPO_POSITION_PNW
53	EVAL_GRP_CN	VARCHAR2(34)	POP_EVAL_GRP.CN
54	EVAL_GRP	NUMBER(6)	POP_EVAL_GRP.EVAL_GRP
55	EXPALL	NUMBER(13,4)	POP_STRATUM.EXPNS
56	EXPCURR	NUMBER(13,4)	POP_STRATUM.EXPNS
57	EXPVOL	NUMBER(13,4)	POP_STRATUM.EXPNS
58	EXPGROW	NUMBER(13,4)	POP_STRATUM.EXPNS
59	EXPMORT	NUMBER(13,4)	POP_STRATUM.EXPNS
60	EXPREMV	NUMBER(13,4)	POP_STRATUM.EXPNS
61	ADJ_EXPALL	NUMBER(5,4)	POP_STRATUM.ADJ_MACR if value of COND.PROP_BASIS equals 'MACR' else from POP_STRATUM.ADJ_SUBP
62	ADJ_EXPCURR	NUMBER(5,4)	POP_STRATUM.ADJ_MACR if value of COND.PROP_BASIS equals 'MACR' else from POP_STRATUM.ADJ_SUBP
63	ADJ_EXPVOL_MACR	NUMBER(5,4)	POP_STRATUM.ADJ_FACTOR_MACR
64	ADJ_EXPVOL_SUBP	NUMBER(5,4)	POP_STRATUM.ADJ_FACTOR_SUBP
65	ADJ_EXPVOL_MICR	NUMBER(5,4)	POP_STRATUM.ADJ_FACTOR_MICR
66	ADJ_EXPGROW_MACR	NUMBER(5,4)	POP_STRATUM.ADJ_FACTOR_MACR
67	ADJ_EXPGROW_SUBP	NUMBER(5,4)	POP_STRATUM.ADJ_FACTOR_SUBP
68	ADJ_EXPGROW_MICR	NUMBER(5,4)	POP_STRATUM.ADJ_FACTOR_MICR
69	ADJ_EXPMORT_MACR	NUMBER(5,4)	POP_STRATUM.ADJ_FACTOR_MACR
70	ADJ_EXPMORT_SUBP	NUMBER(5,4)	POP_STRATUM.ADJ_FACTOR_SUBP
71	ADJ_EXPMORT_MICR	NUMBER(5,4)	POP_STRATUM.ADJ_FACTOR_MICR
72	ADJ_EXPREMV_MACR	NUMBER(5,4)	POP_STRATUM.ADJ_FACTOR_MACR
73	ADJ_EXPREMV_SUBP	NUMBER(5,4)	POP_STRATUM.ADJ_FACTOR_SUBP
74	ADJ_EXPREMV_MICR	NUMBER(5,4)	POP_STRATUM.ADJ_FACTOR_MICR

Variable definitions for the first 52 PLOTSNAP variables can be found in the FIADB 3.0 Users Guide.

53.	EVAL_GRP_CN	Evaluation group control number. Foreign key linking the PLOTSNAP record to a unique POP_EVAL_GRP record.
54.	EVAL_GRP	Evaluation group. A variable that in conjunction with the statecd variable uniquely identifies a unique POP_EVAL_GRP record.
55.	EXPALL	Area expansion factor for all land. The number of acres the sample plot represents for estimating current land area, where the sample includes denied-access and hazardous plots, but excludes outside-of-the-population plots.
56.	EXPCURR	Area expansion factor for forest land and timberland. The number of acres the sample plot represents for estimating current forest and timberland area, where the sample excludes outside-of-the-population, denied-access, and hazardous plots.
57.	EXPVOL	Volume expansion factor for forest land and timberland. The number of acres the sample plot represents for estimating current volume, biomass, and number of trees (based on number of sampled plots only).
58.	EXPGROW	Growth expansion factor for forest land and timberland. The number of acres the sample plot represents for estimating net average annual growth (based on number of sampled plots only).
59.	EXPMORT	Mortality expansion factor for forest land and timberland. The number of acres the sample plot represents for estimating average annual mortality (based on number of sampled plots only).
60.	EXPREMV	Removals expansion factor for forest land and timberland. The number of acres the sample plot represents for estimating average annual removals (based on number of sampled plots only).
61.	ADJ_EXPALL	Adjustment factor for all land area. This adjustment factor should be applied to the CONDPROP_UNADJ on the condition record when generating population estimates to take into account "out of population" portions of conditions within the stratum.
62.	ADJ_EXPCURR	Adjustment factor for forest land and timberland area. This adjustment factor should be applied to the CONDPROP_UNADJ on the condition record when generating population estimates to take into account "out of population" and "denied access/hazardous" portions of conditions within the stratum.

63. ADJ_EXPVOL_MACRO

This adjustment factor should be applied to the TPA_ UNADJ on the tree record when generating population estimates to take into account "out of population" and "denied access/hazardous" portions of conditions within the stratum. This should be applied only to those trees that were measured on the macroplot. Includes trees whose diameters exceed that specified in COND.MACRO_ BREAKPOINT_DIA when MACRO_BREAKPOINT_ DIA is not null.

64. ADJ_EXPVOL_SUBP

This adjustment factor should be applied to the TPA_ UNADJ on the tree record when generating population estimates to take into account "out of population" and "denied access/hazardous" portions of conditions within the stratum. This should be applied only to those trees that were measured on the subplot.

65. ADJ_EXPVOL_MICR

This adjustment factor should be applied to the TPA_ UNADJ on the tree record when generating population estimates to take into account "out of population" and "denied access/hazardous" portions of conditions within the stratum. This should be applied only to those trees that were measured on the microplot. Includes trees from 1.00 to 4.99 inches d.b.h.

66. ADJ_EXPGROW_MACRO

This adjustment factor should be applied to the TPAGROW_UNADJ on the tree record when generating population estimates to take into account "out of population" and "denied access/hazardous" portions of conditions within the stratum. This should be applied only to those trees that were measured on the macroplot. Includes trees whose diameters exceed that specified in COND.MACRO_BREAKPOINT_DIA when MACRO_ BREAKPOINT_DIA is not null.

67. ADJ_EXPGROW_SUBP

This adjustment factor should be applied to the TPAGROW_UNADJ on the tree record when generating population estimates to take into account "out of population" and "denied access/hazardous" portions of conditions within the stratum. This should be applied only to those trees that were measured on the subplot.

68. ADJ_EXPGROW_MICR

This adjustment factor should be applied to the TPAGROW_UNADJ on the tree record when generating population estimates to take into account "out of population" and "denied access/hazardous" portions of conditions within the stratum. This should be applied only to those trees that were measured on the microplot. Includes trees from 1.00 to 4.99 inches d.b.h.

69. ADJ_EXPMORT_MACRO This adjustment factor should be applied to the TPAMORT_UNADJ on the tree record when generating population estimates to take into account "out of population" and "denied access/hazardous" portions of conditions within the stratum. This should be applied only to those trees that were measured on the macroplot. Includes trees whose diameters exceed that specified in COND.MACRO_BREAKPOINT_DIA when MACRO_BREAKPOINT_DIA is not null.

70. ADJ_EXPMORT_SUBP This adjustment factor should be applied to the TPAMORT_UNADJ on the tree record when generating population estimates to take into account "out of population" and "denied access/hazardous" portions of conditions within the stratum. This should be applied only to those trees that were measured on the subplot.

71. ADJ_EXPMORT_MICR This adjustment factor should be applied to the TPAMORT_UNADJ on the tree record when generating population estimates to take into account "out of population" and "denied access/hazardous" portions of conditions within the stratum. This should be applied only to those trees that were measured on the microplot. Includes trees from 1.00 to 4.99 inches d.b.h.

72. ADJ_EXPREMV_MACRO This adjustment factor should be applied to the TPAREMV_UNADJ on the tree record when generating population estimates to take into account "out of population" and "denied access/hazardous" portions of conditions within the stratum. This should be applied only to those trees that were measured on the macroplot. Trees whose diameters exceed that specified in COND.MACRO_BREAKPOINT_DIA when MACRO_BREAKPOINT_DIA is not null.

73. ADJ_EXPREMV_SUBP This adjustment factor should be applied to the TPAREMV_UNADJ on the tree record when generating population estimates to take into account "out of population" and "denied access/hazardous" portions of conditions within the stratum. This should be applied only to those trees that were measured on the subplot.

74. ADJ_EXPREMV_MICR This adjustment factor should be applied to the TPAREMV_UNADJ on the tree record when generating population estimates to take into account "out of population" and "denied access/hazardous" portions of conditions within the stratum. This should be applied only to those trees that were measured on the microplot. Includes trees from 1.00 to 4.99 inches d.b.h.

APPENDIX B—EXAMPLE ORACLE SQL SCRIPTS FOR GENERATING POPULATION ESTIMATES

ATTRIBUTE_DESCR	Calculations

Area sampled and denied access hazardous(acres)	**select** peg.eval_grp_descr,
	
	    sum(c.condprop_unadj * expall* adj_expall) units
	
	  from pop_eval_grp peg, plotsnap p, cond c
	
	where p.cn = c.plt_cn
	
	  and peg.eval_grp = p.eval_grp
	
	  and peg.statecd = p.statecd
	
	  and peg.statecd = 27 and peg.eval_grp = 272005
	
	group by peg.eval_grp_descr;

Area of forest land(acres)	**select** peg.eval_grp_descr,
	
	    sum(c.condprop_unadj * expcurr * adj_expcurr) units
	
	  from pop_eval_grp peg, plotsnap p, cond c
	
	where c.cond_status_cd = 1
	
	  and p.cn = c.plt_cn
	
	  and peg.eval_grp = p.eval_grp
	
	  and peg.statecd = p.statecd
	
	  and peg.statecd = 27 and peg.eval_grp = 272005
	
	group by peg.eval_grp_descr;

Area of timberland(acres)	**select** peg.eval_grp_descr,
	
	    sum(c.condprop_unadj * expcurr * adj_expcurr) units
	
	  from pop_eval_grp peg, plotsnap p, cond c
	
	where c.cond_status_cd = 1
	
	  and c.reservcd = 0
	
	  and c.siteclcd **in** (1, 2, 3, 4, 5, 6)
	
	  and p.cn = c.plt_cn
	
	  and peg.eval_grp = p.eval_grp
	
	  and peg.statecd = p.statecd
	
	  and peg.statecd = 27 and peg.eval_grp = 272005
	
	group by peg.eval_grp_descr;

Number of all live trees on forest land(trees)	**select** peg.eval_grp_descr,
	    sum(t.tpa_unadj * expvol *
	    decode(dia,null,adj_expvol_subp,
	        decode(least(dia,5-0.001),dia,adj_expvol_micr,
	        decode(least(dia,
	        nvl(MACRO_BREAKPOINT_DIA,9999)- 0.001),
	        dia,adj_expvol_subp,
	        adj_expvol_macr)))) units
	 from pop_eval_grp peg, plotsnap p, cond c, tree t
	where t.plt_cn = c.plt_cn
	 and t.condid = c.condid
	 and c.cond_status_cd = 1
	 and t.statuscd = 1
	 and t.dia >= 1.0
	 and p.cn = c.plt_cn
	 and peg.eval_grp = p.eval_grp
	 and peg.statecd = p.statecd
	 and peg.statecd = 27 and peg.eval_grp = 272005
	group by peg.eval_grp_descr;

Number of growing-stock trees on forest land(trees)	**select** peg.eval_grp_descr,
	    sum(t.tpa_unadj * expvol *
	    decode(dia,null,adj_expvol_subp,
	        decode(least(dia,5-0.001),dia,adj_expvol_micr,
	        decode(least(dia,
	        nvl(MACRO_BREAKPOINT_DIA,9999)- 0.001),
	        dia,adj_expvol_subp,
	        adj_expvol_macr)))) units
	 from pop_eval_grp peg, plotsnap p, cond c, tree t
	where t.plt_cn = c.plt_cn
	 and t.condid = c.condid
	 and c.cond_status_cd = 1
	 and t.statuscd = 1
	 and t.treeclcd = 2
	 and t.dia >= 1.0
	 and p.cn = c.plt_cn
	 and peg.eval_grp = p.eval_grp
	 and peg.statecd = p.statecd
	 and peg.statecd = 27 and peg.eval_grp = 272005
	group by peg.eval_grp_descr;

Number of standing dead trees 5"+ d.b.h. on forest land(trees)	**select** peg.eval_grp_descr,
	    sum(t.tpa_unadj * expvol *
	    decode(dia,null,adj_expvol_subp,
	        decode(least(dia,5-0.001),dia,adj_expvol_micr,
	        decode(least(dia,
	        nvl(MACRO_BREAKPOINT_DIA,9999)- 0.001),
	        dia,adj_expvol_subp,
	        adj_expvol_macr)))) units
	  from pop_eval_grp peg, plotsnap p, cond c, tree t
	where t.plt_cn = c.plt_cn
	  and t.condid = c.condid
	  and c.cond_status_cd = 1
	  and t.statuscd = 2
	  and t.standing_dead_cd = 1
	  and t.dia >= 5.0
	  and p.cn = c.plt_cn
	  and peg.eval_grp = p.eval_grp
	  and peg.statecd = p.statecd
	  and peg.statecd = 27 and peg.eval_grp = 272005
	  group by peg.eval_grp_descr;

Number of all live trees on timberland(trees)	**select** peg.eval_grp_descr,
	    sum(t.tpa_unadj * expvol *
	    decode(dia,null,adj_expvol_subp,
	        decode(least(dia,5-0.001),dia,adj_expvol_micr,
	        decode(least(dia,
	        nvl(MACRO_BREAKPOINT_DIA,9999)- 0.001),
	        dia,adj_expvol_subp,
	        adj_expvol_macr)))) units
	  from pop_eval_grp peg, plotsnap p, cond c, tree t
	where t.plt_cn = c.plt_cn
	  and t.condid = c.condid
	  and c.cond_status_cd = 1
	  and c.reservcd = 0
	  and c.siteclcd in (1, 2, 3, 4, 5, 6)
	  and t.statuscd = 1
	  and t.dia >= 1.0
	  and p.cn = c.plt_cn
	  and peg.eval_grp = p.eval_grp
	  and peg.statecd = p.statecd
	  and peg.statecd = 27 and peg.eval_grp = 272005
	  group by peg.eval_grp_descr;

Number of growing-stock trees on timberland(trees)	**select** peg.eval_grp_descr,
	   sum(t.tpa_unadj * expvol *
	   decode(dia,null,adj_expvol_subp,
	      decode(least(dia,5-0.001),dia,adj_expvol_micr,
	      decode(least(dia,
	     nvl(MACRO_BREAKPOINT_DIA,9999)- 0.001),
	     dia,adj_expvol_subp,
	     adj_expvol_macr)))) units
	 from pop_eval_grp peg, plotsnap p, cond c, tree t
	where t.plt_cn = c.plt_cn
	 and t.condid = c.condid
	 and c.cond_status_cd = 1
	 and c.reservcd = 0
	 and c.siteclcd in (1, 2, 3, 4, 5, 6)
	 and t.statuscd = 1
	 and t.treeclcd = 2
	 and t.dia >= 1.0
	 and p.cn = c.plt_cn
	 and peg.eval_grp = p.eval_grp
	 and peg.statecd = p.statecd
	 and peg.statecd = 27 and peg.eval_grp = 272005
	group by peg.eval_grp_descr;

Number of standing dead trees 5″+ d.b.h. on timberland(trees)	**select** peg.eval_grp_descr,
	    sum(t.tpa_unadj * expvol *
	    decode(dia,null,adj_expvol_subp,
	        decode(least(dia,5-0.001),dia,adj_expvol_micr,
	        decode(least(dia,
	      nvl(MACRO_BREAKPOINT_DIA,9999)- 0.001),
	      dia,adj_expvol_subp,
	      adj_expvol_macr)))) units
	 from pop_eval_grp peg, plotsnap p, cond c, tree t
	where t.plt_cn = c.plt_cn
	 and t.condid = c.condid
	 and c.cond_status_cd = 1
	 and c.reservcd = 0
	 and c.siteclcd in (1, 2, 3, 4, 5, 6)
	 and t.statuscd = 2
	 and t.standing_dead_cd = 1
	 and t.dia >= 5.0
	 and p.cn = c.plt_cn
	 and peg.eval_grp = p.eval_grp
	 and peg.statecd = p.statecd
	 and peg.statecd = 27 and peg.eval_grp = 272005
	group by peg.eval_grp_descr;

All live biomass on forest land oven-dry(tons)	**select** peg.eval_grp_descr,
	    sum(t.tpa_unadj * t.drybiot / 2000 * expvol *
	    decode(dia,null,adj_expvol_subp,
	        decode(least(dia,5-0.001),dia,adj_expvol_micr,
	        decode(least(dia,
	      nvl(MACRO_BREAKPOINT_DIA,9999)- 0.001),
	      dia,adj_expvol_subp,
	      adj_expvol_macr)))) units
	 from pop_eval_grp peg, plotsnap p, cond c, tree t
	where t.plt_cn = c.plt_cn
	 and t.condid = c.condid
	 and c.cond_status_cd = 1
	 and t.statuscd = 1
	 and p.cn = c.plt_cn
	 and peg.eval_grp = p.eval_grp
	 and peg.statecd = p.statecd
	 and peg.statecd = 27 and peg.eval_grp = 272005
	group by peg.eval_grp_descr;

All live merchantable tree biomass on forest land oven-dry(tons)	**select** peg.eval_grp_descr,
	    sum(t.tpa_unadj * t.drybiom / 2000 * expvol *
	    decode(dia,null,adj_expvol_subp,
	        decode(least(dia,5-0.001),dia,adj_expvol_micr,
	        decode(least(dia,
	        nvl(MACRO_BREAKPOINT_DIA,9999)- 0.001),
	        dia,adj_expvol_subp,
	        adj_expvol_macr)))) units
	  from pop_eval_grp peg, plotsnap p, cond c, tree t
	  where t.plt_cn = c.plt_cn
	   and t.condid = c.condid
	   and c.cond_status_cd = 1
	   and t.statuscd = 1
	   and p.cn = c.plt_cn
	   and peg.eval_grp = p.eval_grp
	   and peg.statecd = p.statecd
	   and peg.statecd = 27 and peg.eval_grp = 272005
	  group by peg.eval_grp_descr;

All live merchantable tree biomass on timberland oven-dry(tons)	**select** peg.eval_grp_descr,
	    sum(t.tpa_unadj * t.drybiom / 2000 * expvol *
	    decode(dia,null,adj_expvol_subp,
	        decode(least(dia,5-0.001),dia,adj_expvol_micr,
	        decode(least(dia,
	        nvl(MACRO_BREAKPOINT_DIA,9999)- 0.001),
	        dia,adj_expvol_subp,
	        adj_expvol_macr)))) units
	  from pop_eval_grp peg, plotsnap p, cond c, tree t
	  where t.plt_cn = c.plt_cn
	   and t.condid = c.condid
	   and c.cond_status_cd = 1
	   and c.reservcd = 0
	   and c.siteclcd in (1, 2, 3, 4, 5, 6)
	   and t.statuscd = 1
	   and p.cn = c.plt_cn
	   and peg.eval_grp = p.eval_grp
	   and peg.statecd = p.statecd
	   and peg.statecd = 27 and peg.eval_grp = 272005
	  group by peg.eval_grp_descr;

All live tree biomass on timberland oven-dry (tons)	select peg.eval_grp_descr,
	
	    sum(t.tpa_unadj * t.drybiot / 2000 * expvol *
	
	    decode(dia,null,adj_expvol_subp,
	
	        decode(least(dia,5-0.001),dia,adj_expvol_micr,
	
	        decode(least(dia,
	
	      nvl(MACRO_BREAKPOINT_DIA,9999)- 0.001),
	
	      dia,adj_expvol_subp,
	
	      adj_expvol_macr)))) units
	
	 from pop_eval_grp peg, plotsnap p, cond c, tree t
	
	where t.plt_cn = c.plt_cn
	
	 and t.condid = c.condid
	
	 and c.cond_status_cd = 1
	
	 and c.reservcd = 0
	
	 and c.siteclcd in (1, 2, 3, 4, 5, 6)
	
	 and t.statuscd = 1
	
	 and p.cn = c.plt_cn
	
	 and peg.eval_grp = p.eval_grp
	
	 and peg.statecd = p.statecd
	
	 and peg.statecd = 27 and peg.eval_grp = 272005
	
	 group by peg.eval_grp_descr;

Volume of all live trees on forest land(cuft)	select peg.eval_grp_descr,
	
	    sum(t.tpa_unadj * t.volcfnet * expvol *
	
	    decode(dia,null,adj_expvol_subp,
	
	        decode(least(dia,5-0.001),dia,adj_expvol_micr,
	
	        decode(least(dia,
	
	      nvl(MACRO_BREAKPOINT_DIA,9999)- 0.001),
	
	      dia,adj_expvol_subp,
	
	      adj_expvol_macr)))) units
	
	 from pop_eval_grp peg, plotsnap p, cond c, tree t
	
	where t.plt_cn = c.plt_cn
	
	 and t.condid = c.condid
	
	 and c.cond_status_cd = 1
	
	 and t.statuscd = 1
	
	 and p.cn = c.plt_cn
	
	 and peg.eval_grp = p.eval_grp
	
	 and peg.statecd = p.statecd
	
	 and peg.statecd = 27 and peg.eval_grp = 272005
	
	 group by peg.eval_grp_descr;

Volume of growing stock on forest land(cuft)	**select** peg.eval_grp_descr,
	    sum(t.tpa_unadj * t.volcfnet * expvol *
	    decode(dia,null,adj_expvol_subp,
	        decode(least(dia,5-0.001),dia,adj_expvol_micr,
	        decode(least(dia,
	        nvl(MACRO_BREAKPOINT_DIA,9999)- 0.001),
	        dia,adj_expvol_subp,
	        adj_expvol_macr)))) units
	  from pop_eval_grp peg, plotsnap p, cond c, tree t
	  where t.plt_cn = c.plt_cn
	  and t.condid = c.condid
	  and c.cond_status_cd = 1
	  and t.statuscd = 1
	  and t.treeclcd = 2
	  and p.cn = c.plt_cn
	  and peg.eval_grp = p.eval_grp
	  and peg.statecd = p.statecd
	  and peg.statecd = 27 and peg.eval_grp = 272005
	  group by peg.eval_grp_descr;

Volume of sawlog portion on forest land(cuft)	**select** peg.eval_grp_descr,
	    sum(t.tpa_unadj * t.volcsnet * expvol *
	    decode(dia,null,adj_expvol_subp,
	        decode(least(dia,5-0.001),dia,adj_expvol_micr,
	        decode(least(dia,
	        nvl(MACRO_BREAKPOINT_DIA,9999)- 0.001),
	        dia,adj_expvol_subp,
	        adj_expvol_macr)))) units
	  from pop_eval_grp peg, plotsnap p, cond c, tree t
	  where t.plt_cn = c.plt_cn
	  and t.condid = c.condid
	  and c.cond_status_cd = 1
	  and t.statuscd = 1
	  and t.treeclcd = 2
	  and p.cn = c.plt_cn
	  and peg.eval_grp = p.eval_grp
	  and peg.statecd = p.statecd
	  and peg.statecd = 27 and peg.eval_grp = 272005
	  group by peg.eval_grp_descr;

Volume of all live trees on timberland(cuft)	select peg.eval_grp_descr,
	    sum(t.tpa_unadj * t.volcfnet * expvol *
	    decode(dia,null,adj_expvol_subp,
	        decode(least(dia,5-0.001),dia,adj_expvol_micr,
	        decode(least(dia,
	      nvl(MACRO_BREAKPOINT_DIA,9999)- 0.001),
	      dia,adj_expvol_subp,
	      adj_expvol_macr)))) units
	 from pop_eval_grp peg, plotsnap p, cond c, tree t
	where t.plt_cn = c.plt_cn
	 and t.condid = c.condid
	 and c.cond_status_cd = 1
	 and c.reservcd = 0
	 and c.siteclcd in (1, 2, 3, 4, 5, 6)
	 and t.statuscd = 1
	 and p.cn = c.plt_cn
	 and peg.eval_grp = p.eval_grp
	 and peg.statecd = p.statecd
	 and peg.statecd = 27 and peg.eval_grp = 272005
	group by peg.eval_grp_descr;

Volume of growing stock on timberland(cuft)	select peg.eval_grp_descr,
	    sum(t.tpa_unadj * t.volcfnet * expvol *
	    decode(dia,null,adj_expvol_subp,
	        decode(least(dia,5-0.001),dia,adj_expvol_micr,
	        decode(least(dia,
	      nvl(MACRO_BREAKPOINT_DIA,9999)- 0.001),
	      dia,adj_expvol_subp,
	      adj_expvol_macr)))) units
	 from pop_eval_grp peg, plotsnap p, cond c, tree t
	where t.plt_cn = c.plt_cn
	 and t.condid = c.condid
	 and c.cond_status_cd = 1
	 and c.reservcd = 0
	 and c.siteclcd in (1, 2, 3, 4, 5, 6)
	 and t.statuscd = 1
	 and t.treeclcd = 2
	 and p.cn = c.plt_cn
	 and peg.eval_grp = p.eval_grp
	 and peg.statecd = p.statecd
	 and peg.statecd = 27 and peg.eval_grp = 272005
	group by peg.eval_grp_descr;

Volume of sawlog portion on timberland(cuft)	select peg.eval_grp_descr,
	    sum(t.tpa_unadj * t.volcsnet * expvol *
	    decode(dia,null,adj_expvol_subp,
	        decode(least(dia,5-0.001),dia,adj_expvol_micr,
	        decode(least(dia,
	        nvl(MACRO_BREAKPOINT_DIA,9999)- 0.001),
	        dia,adj_expvol_subp,
	        adj_expvol_macr)))) units
	 from pop_eval_grp peg, plotsnap p, cond c, tree t
	where t.plt_cn = c.plt_cn
	 and t.condid = c.condid
	 and c.cond_status_cd = 1
	 and c.reservcd = 0
	 and c.siteclcd in (1, 2, 3, 4, 5, 6)
	 and t.statuscd = 1
	 and t.treeclcd = 2
	 and p.cn = c.plt_cn
	 and peg.eval_grp = p.eval_grp
	 and peg.statecd = p.statecd
	 and peg.statecd = 27 and peg.eval_grp = 272005
	 group by peg.eval_grp_descr;

Volume of sawtimber on forest land(bdft)	select peg.eval_grp_descr,
	    sum(t.tpa_unadj * t.volbfnet * expvol *
	    decode(dia,null,adj_expvol_subp,
	        decode(least(dia,5-0.001),dia,adj_expvol_micr,
	        decode(least(dia,
	        nvl(MACRO_BREAKPOINT_DIA,9999)- 0.001),
	        dia,adj_expvol_subp,
	        adj_expvol_macr)))) units
	 from pop_eval_grp peg, plotsnap p, cond c, tree t
	where t.plt_cn = c.plt_cn
	 and t.condid = c.condid
	 and c.cond_status_cd = 1
	 and t.statuscd = 1
	 and t.treeclcd = 2
	 and p.cn = c.plt_cn
	 and peg.eval_grp = p.eval_grp
	 and peg.statecd = p.statecd
	 and peg.statecd = 27 and peg.eval_grp = 272005
	 group by peg.eval_grp_descr;

Volume of sawtimber on timberland(bdft)	**select** peg.eval_grp_descr,
	    sum(t.tpa_unadj * t.volbfnet * expvol *
	    decode(dia,null,adj_expvol_subp,
	        decode(least(dia,5-0.001),dia,adj_expvol_micr,
	        decode(least(dia,
	      nvl(MACRO_BREAKPOINT_DIA,9999)- 0.001),
	      dia,adj_expvol_subp,
	      adj_expvol_macr)))) units
	 from pop_eval_grp peg, plotsnap p, cond c, tree t
	 where t.plt_cn = c.plt_cn
	  and t.condid = c.condid
	  and c.cond_status_cd = 1
	  and c.reservcd = 0
	  and c.siteclcd in (1, 2, 3, 4, 5, 6)
	  and t.statuscd = 1
	  and t.treeclcd = 2
	  and p.cn = c.plt_cn
	  and peg.eval_grp = p.eval_grp
	  and peg.statecd = p.statecd
	  and peg.statecd = 27 and peg.eval_grp = 272005
	 group by peg.eval_grp_descr;

All live gross sawtimber volume on forest land(bdft)	**select** peg.eval_grp_descr,
	    sum(t.tpa_unadj * volbfgrs * expvol *
	    decode(dia,null,adj_expvol_subp,
	        decode(least(dia,5-0.001),dia,adj_expvol_micr,
	        decode(least(dia,
	      nvl(MACRO_BREAKPOINT_DIA,9999)- 0.001),
	      dia,adj_expvol_subp,
	      adj_expvol_macr)))) units
	 from pop_eval_grp peg, plotsnap p, cond c, tree t
	 where t.plt_cn = c.plt_cn
	  and t.condid = c.condid
	  and c.cond_status_cd = 1
	  and t.statuscd = 1
	  and p.cn = c.plt_cn
	  and peg.eval_grp = p.eval_grp
	  and peg.statecd = p.statecd
	  and peg.statecd = 27 and peg.eval_grp = 272005
	 group by peg.eval_grp_descr;

All live tree gross volume on forest land(cuft)	**select** peg.eval_grp_descr,
	    sum(t.tpa_unadj * volcfgrs * expvol *
	    decode(dia,null,adj_expvol_subp,
	        decode(least(dia,5-0.001),dia,adj_expvol_micr,
	        decode(least(dia,
	        nvl(MACRO_BREAKPOINT_DIA,9999)- 0.001),
	        dia,adj_expvol_subp,
	        adj_expvol_macr)))) units
	  from pop_eval_grp peg, plotsnap p, cond c, tree t
	  where t.plt_cn = c.plt_cn
	   and t.condid = c.condid
	   and c.cond_status_cd = 1
	   and t.statuscd = 1
	   and p.cn = c.plt_cn
	   and peg.eval_grp = p.eval_grp
	   and peg.statecd = p.statecd
	   and peg.statecd = 27 and peg.eval_grp = 272005
	  group by peg.eval_grp_descr;

All live tree sound volume on forest land(cuft)	**select** peg.eval_grp_descr,
	    sum(t.tpa_unadj * volcfsnd * expvol *
	    decode(dia,null,adj_expvol_subp,
	        decode(least(dia,5-0.001),dia,adj_expvol_micr,
	        decode(least(dia,
	        nvl(MACRO_BREAKPOINT_DIA,9999)- 0.001),
	        dia,adj_expvol_subp,
	        adj_expvol_macr)))) units
	  from pop_eval_grp peg, plotsnap p, cond c, tree t
	  where t.plt_cn = c.plt_cn
	   and t.condid = c.condid
	   and c.cond_status_cd = 1
	   and t.statuscd = 1
	   and p.cn = c.plt_cn
	   and peg.eval_grp = p.eval_grp
	   and peg.statecd = p.statecd
	   and peg.statecd = 27 and peg.eval_grp = 272005
	  group by peg.eval_grp_descr;

Net growth of all live trees on forest land(cuft per year)	select peg.eval_grp_descr,
	
	    sum(t.tpagrow_unadj * fgrowcfal * expgrow *
	
	    decode(dia,null,adj_expgrow_subp,
	
	        decode(least(dia,5-0.001),dia,adj_expgrow_micr,
	
	        decode(least(dia,
	
	        nvl(MACRO_BREAKPOINT_DIA,9999)- 0.001),
	
	        dia,adj_expgrow_subp,
	
	        adj_expgrow_macr)))) units
	
	  from pop_eval_grp peg, plotsnap p, cond c, tree t
	
	  where t.plt_cn = c.plt_cn
	
	   and t.condid = c.condid
	
	   and p.cn = c.plt_cn
	
	   and peg.eval_grp = p.eval_grp
	
	   and peg.statecd = p.statecd
	
	   and peg.statecd = 27 and peg.eval_grp = 272005
	
	  group by peg.eval_grp_descr;

Net growth of growing stock on forest land(cuft per year)	select peg.eval_grp_descr,
	
	    sum(t.tpagrow_unadj * fgrowcfgs * expgrow *
	
	    decode(dia,null,adj_expgrow_subp,
	
	        decode(least(dia,5-0.001),dia,adj_expgrow_micr,
	
	        decode(least(dia,
	
	        nvl(MACRO_BREAKPOINT_DIA,9999)- 0.001),
	
	        dia,adj_expgrow_subp,
	
	        adj_expgrow_macr)))) units
	
	  from pop_eval_grp peg, plotsnap p, cond c, tree t
	
	  where t.plt_cn = c.plt_cn
	
	   and t.condid = c.condid
	
	   and p.cn = c.plt_cn
	
	   and peg.eval_grp = p.eval_grp
	
	   and peg.statecd = p.statecd
	
	   and peg.statecd = 27 and peg.eval_grp = 272005
	
	  group by peg.eval_grp_descr;

| **Net growth of sawtimber on forest land(bdft per year)** | ```
select peg.eval_grp_descr,
    sum(t.tpagrow_unadj * fgrowbfsl * expgrow *
    decode(dia,null,adj_expgrow_subp,
        decode(least(dia,5-0.001),dia,adj_expgrow_micr,
        decode(least(dia,
        nvl(MACRO_BREAKPOINT_DIA,9999)-   0.001),
        dia,adj_expgrow_subp,
        adj_expgrow_macr)))) units
 from pop_eval_grp peg, plotsnap p, cond c, tree t
 where t.plt_cn = c.plt_cn
  and t.condid = c.condid
  and p.cn = c.plt_cn
  and peg.eval_grp = p.eval_grp
  and peg.statecd = p.statecd
  and peg.statecd = 27 and peg.eval_grp = 272005
 group by  peg.eval_grp_descr;
``` |
| **Net growth of all live trees on timberland(cuft per year)** | ```
select peg.eval_grp_descr,
    sum(t.tpagrow_unadj * growcfal * expgrow *
    decode(dia,null,adj_expgrow_subp,
        decode(least(dia,5-0.001),dia,adj_expgrow_micr,
        decode(least(dia,
        nvl(MACRO_BREAKPOINT_DIA,9999)-   0.001),
        dia,adj_expgrow_subp,
        adj_expgrow_macr)))) units
 from pop_eval_grp peg, plotsnap p, cond c, tree t
 where t.plt_cn = c.plt_cn
  and t.condid = c.condid
  and p.cn = c.plt_cn
  and peg.eval_grp = p.eval_grp
  and peg.statecd = p.statecd
  and peg.statecd = 27 and peg.eval_grp = 272005
 group by  peg.eval_grp_descr;
``` |

Net growth of growing stock on timberland(cuft per year)	select peg.eval_grp_descr,
	    sum(t.tpagrow_unadj * t.growcfgs * expgrow *
	    decode(dia,null,adj_expgrow_subp,
	        decode(least(dia,5-0.001),dia,adj_expgrow_micr,
	        decode(least(dia,
	        nvl(MACRO_BREAKPOINT_DIA,9999)- 0.001),
	        dia,adj_expgrow_subp,
	        adj_expgrow_macr)))) units
	 from pop_eval_grp peg, plotsnap p, cond c, tree t
	 where t.plt_cn = c.plt_cn
	  and t.condid = c.condid
	  and p.cn = c.plt_cn
	  and peg.eval_grp = p.eval_grp
	  and peg.statecd = p.statecd
	  and peg.statecd = 27 and peg.eval_grp = 272005
	 group by peg.eval_grp_descr;

Net growth of sawtimber on timberland(bdft per year)	select peg.eval_grp_descr,
	    sum(t.tpagrow_unadj * t.growbfsl * expgrow *
	    decode(dia,null,adj_expgrow_subp,
	        decode(least(dia,5-0.001),dia,adj_expgrow_micr,
	        decode(least(dia,
	        nvl(MACRO_BREAKPOINT_DIA,9999)- 0.001),
	        dia,adj_expgrow_subp,
	        adj_expgrow_macr)))) units
	 from pop_eval_grp peg, plotsnap p, cond c, tree t
	 where t.plt_cn = c.plt_cn
	  and t.condid = c.condid
	  and p.cn = c.plt_cn
	  and peg.eval_grp = p.eval_grp
	  and peg.statecd = p.statecd
	  and peg.statecd = 27 and peg.eval_grp = 272005
	 group by peg.eval_grp_descr;

Mortality of all live trees on forest land(cuft per year)	**select** peg.eval_grp_descr,
	    sum(t.tpamort_unadj * fmortcfal * expmort *
	    decode(dia,null,adj_expmort_subp,
	        decode(least(dia,5-0.001),dia,adj_expmort_micr,
	        decode(least(dia,
	        nvl(MACRO_BREAKPOINT_DIA,9999)- 0.001),
	        dia,adj_expmort_subp,
	        adj_expmort_macr)))) units
	  from pop_eval_grp peg, plotsnap p, cond c, tree t
	  where t.plt_cn = c.plt_cn
	  and t.condid = c.condid
	  and p.cn = c.plt_cn
	  and peg.eval_grp = p.eval_grp
	  and peg.statecd = p.statecd
	  and peg.statecd = 27 and peg.eval_grp = 272005
	  group by peg.eval_grp_descr;

Mortality of all live trees on forest land(trees per year)	**select** peg.eval_grp_descr,
	    sum(t.tpamort_unadj * expmort *
	    decode(dia,null,adj_expmort_subp,
	        decode(least(dia,5-0.001),dia,adj_expmort_micr,
	        decode(least(dia,
	        nvl(MACRO_BREAKPOINT_DIA,9999)- 0.001),
	        dia,adj_expmort_subp,
	        adj_expmort_macr)))) units
	  from pop_eval_grp peg, plotsnap p, cond c, tree t
	  where t.plt_cn = c.plt_cn
	  and t.condid = c.condid
	  and p.cn = c.plt_cn
	  and peg.eval_grp = p.eval_grp
	  and peg.statecd = p.statecd
	  and peg.statecd = 27 and peg.eval_grp = 272005
	  group by peg.eval_grp_descr;

Mortality of growing stock on forest land(cuft per year)	**select** peg.eval_grp_descr,
	    sum(t.tpamort_unadj * fmortcfgs * expmort *
	    decode(dia,null,adj_expmort_subp,
	        decode(least(dia,5-0.001),dia,adj_expmort_micr,
	        decode(least(dia,
	        nvl(MACRO_BREAKPOINT_DIA,9999)- 0.001),
	        dia,adj_expmort_subp,
	        adj_expmort_macr)))) units
	  from pop_eval_grp peg, plotsnap p, cond c, tree t
	  where t.plt_cn = c.plt_cn
	   and t.condid = c.condid
	   and p.cn = c.plt_cn
	   and peg.eval_grp = p.eval_grp
	   and peg.statecd = p.statecd
	   and peg.statecd = 27 and peg.eval_grp = 272005
	  group by peg.eval_grp_descr;

Mortality of sawtimber on forest land(cuft per year)	**select** peg.eval_grp_descr,
	    sum(t.tpamort_unadj * fmortbfsl * expmort *
	    decode(dia,null,adj_expmort_subp,
	        decode(least(dia,5-0.001),dia,adj_expmort_micr,
	        decode(least(dia,
	        nvl(MACRO_BREAKPOINT_DIA,9999)- 0.001),
	        dia,adj_expmort_subp,
	        adj_expmort_macr)))) units
	  from pop_eval_grp peg, plotsnap p, cond c, tree t
	  where t.plt_cn = c.plt_cn
	   and t.condid = c.condid
	   and p.cn = c.plt_cn
	   and peg.eval_grp = p.eval_grp
	   and peg.statecd = p.statecd
	   and peg.statecd = 27 and peg.eval_grp = 272005
	  group by peg.eval_grp_descr;

Mortality of all live trees on timberland(cuft per year)	**select** peg.eval_grp_descr,
	
	    sum(t.tpamort_unadj * mortcfal * expmort *
	
	    decode(dia,null,adj_expmort_subp,
	
	        decode(least(dia,5-0.001),dia,adj_expmort_micr,
	
	        decode(least(dia,
	
	        nvl(MACRO_BREAKPOINT_DIA,9999)- 0.001),
	
	        dia,adj_expmort_subp,
	
	        adj_expmort_macr)))) units
	
	 from pop_eval_grp peg, plotsnap p, cond c, tree t
	
	where t.plt_cn = c.plt_cn
	
	 and t.condid = c.condid
	
	 and p.cn = c.plt_cn
	
	 and peg.eval_grp = p.eval_grp
	
	 and peg.statecd = p.statecd
	
	 and peg.statecd = 27 and peg.eval_grp = 272005
	
	group by peg.eval_grp_descr;

Mortality of all live trees on timberland(trees per year)	**select** peg.eval_grp_descr,
	
	    sum(t.tpamort_unadj * expmort *
	
	    decode(dia,null,adj_expmort_subp,
	
	        decode(least(dia,5-0.001),dia,adj_expmort_micr,
	
	        decode(least(dia,
	
	        nvl(MACRO_BREAKPOINT_DIA,9999)- 0.001),
	
	        dia,adj_expmort_subp,
	
	        adj_expmort_macr)))) units
	
	 from pop_eval_grp peg, plotsnap p, cond c, tree t
	
	where t.plt_cn = c.plt_cn
	
	 and t.condid = c.condid
	
	 and p.cn = c.plt_cn
	
	 and peg.eval_grp = p.eval_grp
	
	 and peg.statecd = p.statecd
	
	 and peg.statecd = 27 and peg.eval_grp = 272005
	
	group by peg.eval_grp_descr;

Mortality of growing stock on timberland(cuft per year)	**select** peg.eval_grp_descr,
	   sum(t.tpamort_unadj * t.mortcfgs * expmort *
	   decode(dia,null,adj_expmort_subp,
	      decode(least(dia,5-0.001),dia,adj_expmort_micr,
	      decode(least(dia,
	      nvl(MACRO_BREAKPOINT_DIA,9999)- 0.001),
	      dia,adj_expmort_subp,
	      adj_expmort_macr)))) units
	 from pop_eval_grp peg, plotsnap p, cond c, tree t
	 where t.plt_cn = c.plt_cn
	  and t.condid = c.condid
	  and p.cn = c.plt_cn
	  and peg.eval_grp = p.eval_grp
	  and peg.statecd = p.statecd
	  and peg.statecd = 27 and peg.eval_grp = 272005
	 group by peg.eval_grp_descr;

Mortality of sawtimber on timberland(bdft per year)	**select** peg.eval_grp_descr,
	   sum(t.tpamort_unadj * t.mortbfsl * expmort *
	   decode(dia,null,adj_expmort_subp,
	      decode(least(dia,5-0.001),dia,adj_expmort_micr,
	      decode(least(dia,
	      nvl(MACRO_BREAKPOINT_DIA,9999)- 0.001),
	      dia,adj_expmort_subp,
	      adj_expmort_macr)))) units
	 from pop_eval_grp peg, plotsnap p, cond c, tree t
	 where t.plt_cn = c.plt_cn
	  and t.condid = c.condid
	  and p.cn = c.plt_cn
	  and peg.eval_grp = p.eval_grp
	  and peg.statecd = p.statecd
	  and peg.statecd = 27 and peg.eval_grp = 272005
	 group by peg.eval_grp_descr;

Removals of all live trees on forest land(cuft per year)	select peg.eval_grp_descr,
	    sum(t.tparemv_unadj * fremvcfal * expremv *
	    decode(dia,null,adj_expremv_subp,
	        decode(least(dia,5-0.001),dia,adj_expremv_micr,
	        decode(least(dia,
	        nvl(MACRO_BREAKPOINT_DIA,9999)- 0.001),
	        dia,adj_expremv_subp,
	        adj_expremv_macr)))) units
	  from pop_eval_grp peg, plotsnap p, cond c, tree t
	  where t.plt_cn = c.plt_cn
	   and t.condid = c.condid
	   and p.cn = c.plt_cn
	   and peg.eval_grp = p.eval_grp
	   and peg.statecd = p.statecd
	   and peg.statecd = 27 and peg.eval_grp = 272005
	  group by peg.eval_grp_descr;

Removals of growing stock on forest land(cuft per year)	select peg.eval_grp_descr,
	    sum(t.tparemv_unadj * fremvcfgs * expremv *
	    decode(dia,null,adj_expremv_subp,
	        decode(least(dia,5-0.001),dia,adj_expremv_micr,
	        decode(least(dia,
	        nvl(MACRO_BREAKPOINT_DIA,9999)- 0.001),
	        dia,adj_expremv_subp,
	        adj_expremv_macr)))) units
	  from pop_eval_grp peg, plotsnap p, cond c, tree t
	  where t.plt_cn = c.plt_cn
	   and t.condid = c.condid
	   and p.cn = c.plt_cn
	   and peg.eval_grp = p.eval_grp
	   and peg.statecd = p.statecd
	   and peg.statecd = 27 and peg.eval_grp = 272005
	  group by peg.eval_grp_descr;

Removals of sawtimber on forest land(cuft per year)	**select** peg.eval_grp_descr,
	    sum(t.tparemv_unadj * fremvbfsl * expremv *
	    decode(dia,null,adj_expremv_subp,
	        decode(least(dia,5-0.001),dia,adj_expremv_micr,
	        decode(least(dia,
	        nvl(MACRO_BREAKPOINT_DIA,9999)- 0.001),
	        dia,adj_expremv_subp,
	        adj_expremv_macr)))) units
	 from pop_eval_grp peg, plotsnap p, cond c, tree t
	where t.plt_cn = c.plt_cn
	 and t.condid = c.condid
	 and p.cn = c.plt_cn
	 and peg.eval_grp = p.eval_grp
	 and peg.statecd = p.statecd
	 and peg.statecd = 27 and peg.eval_grp = 272005
	group by peg.eval_grp_descr;

Removals of all live trees on timberland(cuft per year)	**select** peg.eval_grp_descr,
	    sum(t.tparemv_unadj * remvcfal * expremv *
	    decode(dia,null,adj_expremv_subp,
	        decode(least(dia,5-0.001),dia,adj_expremv_micr,
	        decode(least(dia,
	        nvl(MACRO_BREAKPOINT_DIA,9999)- 0.001),
	        dia,adj_expremv_subp,
	        adj_expremv_macr)))) units
	 from pop_eval_grp peg, plotsnap p, cond c, tree t
	where t.plt_cn = c.plt_cn
	 and t.condid = c.condid
	 and p.cn = c.plt_cn
	 and peg.eval_grp = p.eval_grp
	 and peg.statecd = p.statecd
	 and peg.statecd = 27 and peg.eval_grp = 272005
	group by peg.eval_grp_descr;

| **Removals of growing stock on timberland(cuft per year)** | ```sql
select peg.eval_grp_descr,
     sum(t.tparemv_unadj * t.remvcfgs * expremv *
     decode(dia,null,adj_expremv_subp,
          decode(least(dia,5-0.001),dia,adj_expremv_micr,
          decode(least(dia,
          nvl(MACRO_BREAKPOINT_DIA,9999)-    0.001),
          dia,adj_expremv_subp,
          adj_expremv_macr)))) units
  from pop_eval_grp peg, plotsnap p, cond c, tree t
 where t.plt_cn = c.plt_cn
   and t.condid = c.condid
   and p.cn = c.plt_cn
   and peg.eval_grp = p.eval_grp
   and peg.statecd = p.statecd
   and peg.statecd = 27 and peg.eval_grp = 272005
 group by   peg.eval_grp_descr;
``` |
| **Removals of sawtimber on timberland(bdft per year)** | ```sql
select peg.eval_grp_descr,
     sum(t.tparemv_unadj * t.remvbfsl * expremv *
     decode(dia,null,adj_expremv_subp,
          decode(least(dia,5-0.001),dia,adj_expremv_micr,
          decode(least(dia,
          nvl(MACRO_BREAKPOINT_DIA,9999)-    0.001),
          dia,adj_expremv_subp,
          adj_expremv_macr)))) units
  from pop_eval_grp peg, plotsnap p, cond c, tree t
 where t.plt_cn = c.plt_cn
   and t.condid = c.condid
   and t.treeclcd = 2
   and p.cn = c.plt_cn
   and peg.eval_grp = p.eval_grp
   and peg.statecd = p.statecd
   and peg.statecd = 27 and peg.eval_grp = 272005
 group by   peg.eval_grp_descr;
``` |

www.ingramcontent.com/pod-product-compliance
Lightning Source LLC
Chambersburg PA
CBHW080148300526
45790CB00015B/2916